EGYPTIAN MYTHOLOGY

A Concise Guide to the Ancient Gods and Beliefs

BY

Robert Carlson

© 2016 Copyright

No part of this book may be reproduced in any form or by any electronic or mechanical means including information storage and retrieval systems, without permission in writing from the author.

Table of Contents

Introduction

A Timeline for Ancient Egypt

Historical Egypt

The Myth Of Creation

The Pantheon Of Gods

Mythology In Day To Day Ancient Egypt

The Central Role Of The Temple And Some Temple Rituals

Sources Of The History Of Egyptian Mythology

The Underworld And Life After Death

Pyramids And Their Locations

Conclusion

"As a camel beareth labour, and heat, and hunger and thirst, through deserts of sand, and fainteth not; so the fortitude of man shall sustain him through all perils."

Pharaoh Akhenaton, 18th dynasty

Introduction

The particular geography of Egypt has played a critical role in its history. This can be said of many countries of course, but in Egypt it seems to have had an "undue influence" on its development. A thin land, it is bracketed by Libya and the immense Sahara in the west and the Red Sea, Jordan and Saudi Arabia in the east. In the north it is fringed by the Mediterranean. Unlike in most ancient countries, the people of Egypt, from time immemorial, have been oriented to the north. There lies the Sudan but the main fascination for Egyptians has been the immense river of life, the Nile, that flows from the north and divides the full length of Egypt into two unequal land masses. Known as "the gift of Egypt", the Nile is what made life possible in this otherwise arid land, and it has always supported the existence, development, abundance and mystique of this enduring country. The subject of this publication, Egyptian mythology, has been defined as follows: the belief structure and underlying form of ancient Egyptian culture from circa 3500 BCE to circa 30 BCE.

It is a fascinating and complex story and to appreciate it fully you should refer to the timeline in the next section as you read. More than in other mythologies, the distinction between immortal God and human being was extremely tenuous to the Egyptians; sometimes the characters that populate the story are both an historical human being and a mythological god. The Gods do not dwell in the sky above, as in most other mythologies, but in manmade temples during their lives and then in giant pyramids when they move into the Underworld. For this reason it is essential that in exploring the mythology you should have a reasonable understanding of the real history of the country.

Chapter One

A Timeline for Ancient Egypt

I will make this as brief as possible and only highlight key events. You may even want to skip this section at this point and refer back when you need to orient yourself in the history. Prior to this timeline, Egypt was divided in two: Upper Egypt, represented by a white crown; and Lower Egypt, represented by a Red Crown. Upper Egypt stretched south towards the source of the Nile and was characterized by the desert. Lower Egypt stretched north and was characterized by the rich and fertile land of the Nile Delta, where the mighty river fanned out into many smaller waterways running to the sea. In the Pre-dynastic period, the north defeated the south and the land was united under King Menes, who thereafter wore a double crown to signify the unification. The truth is lost in the mists of time, but of King Menes it has been said that he inherited the throne from the falcon-headed God Horus; he may actually have been the mythical Narmer or Aha; he was the first pharaoh of the first dynasty; and that he ruled circa 3407 to circa 3368 BCE. What does seem to be uncontested fact is that he united Egypt and it is here that we start the timeline.

EARLY DYNASTIC PERIOD c3159 – 2686BCE

1ST AND 2ND DYNASTY

Menes united Upper and Lower Egypt and established Memphis as the capital. This gave him control over the agricultural produce of the Delta and the expanding Levant trading routes. The wealth, influence and power of the pharaohs was established and the rituals and cults around the burial tombs, the mastaba, were inculcated among the population.

THE OLD KINGDOM c2686 – 2181BCE

3RD TO 6TH DYNASTY

The centralized administration supported major developments in several areas. The Great Sphinx and the three Giza pyramids were constructed. Imhotep, a gifted architect, was born in 2667 BCE and was influential to his death in 2600 BCE and beyond. There were developments in medicine, mathematics, literature and technology; for example the development of the ceramic glaze known as faience occurred during this period. A combination of factors brought this productive time to an end; the administration became top-heavy; central authority was challenged from smaller centers and a crippling drought developed from c2200 BCE.

FIRST INTERMEDIATE PERIOD c2181 – 2040BCE

7TH TO MIDWAY THROUGH THE 11TH DYNASTY

Regional governors became less dependent on the pharaohs as provincial areas initially thrived and prospered. As individual families became economically and culturally richer, the inevitable rivalries for political power and land ownership escalated and eventually Lower Egypt was controlled by rulers in Herakleopolis and Upper Egypt was claimed by the Intef clan based in Thebes. Around 2055 BCE a victory by the Theban forces imposed unity again and the destructive era drew to a close. Recent research has revealed that the annual flooding of the Nile was less pronounced during this period.

MIDDLE KINGDOM c2040 – 1786BCE

END OF 11TH AND 12TH DYNASTY

The return of the power of the pharaohs, ruling from Thebes, reinforced former glory and traditions. Sensuret l built the largest temple ever at Karnak in honor of Anum-Re. In what has been called a "democratization of the afterlife" the ordinary population also followed more lavish and ritualized burial procedures; there was also a general increase in religious observance. The pharaohs of the 12th dynasty were quite far-sighted - instead of relying on the annual flooding of the Nile, they began supportive irrigation schemes and extensive reclamation of land, impressively improving the agricultural output. Works started on building a dam to control the flow of water into the Faiyum Depression at Lahum by Pharaoh Senusert ll. Needing more laborers, Amenemhat lll allowed Asiatic settlers into the Delta areas. They also re-conquered land lost in Nubia, including much needed quarries and gold mines. As this golden age drew to a close, inadequate Nile flooding and a strained economy produced tensions and political upheaval; the "settlers" took control of the Delta region and came to power in Egypt as the Hykos.

SECOND INTERMEDIATE PERIOD c1786 – 1567BCE

13TH TO 17TH DYNASTY

This was a period of foreign control in Egypt. The pharaohs were pushed back to Thebes and were harassed by the Hykos, both in the north and by their Nubian allies the Kushites in the south. A war of resistance went on for thirty years until the Hykos were finally defeated by Ahmose l.

THE NEW KINGDOM c1567 – 1069BCE

18TH TO 20TH DYNASTY

Initially, under the military, this was a time of increasing prosperity as Egypt expanded its territory. The Pharaohs Tuthmosis l and ll gradually reintroduced traditional beliefs and supported the influence of the Amun Priests. In 1350 BCE there began an unprecedented upheaval when Amenhotep lV ascended the throne. A devotee of the rather obscure sun-disc God Aten, he promoted the following of Aten to the exclusion off any other God for more than twenty years. He changed his name to Akhenaten and built a new Egyptian capital at Amarna, called Akhetaten. This became known as the Amarna Heresy and it caused much dismay and chaos; Akhenaten even went as far as ordering the destruction of certain temples dedicated to other gods.

The situation was salvaged by the coming of Ramesses ll, known as Ramesses the Great, to the throne in 1279 BCE. Once again the people were encouraged to honor all the gods and to have freedom of choice in terms of who they followed. Ramesses the Great steadily increased the wealth of Egypt by successful military campaigns. He is also credited with making the first written peace treaty ever recorded, which was signed with the Hittites in 1258BCE after both sides acknowledged a stalemate in the wake of the Battle of Kardesh. The immense accumulation of wealth led to increasing invasions from external enemies. There were also increasing domestic problems with corruption, tomb robbery and civil unrest as this period drew to an uneasy close. This would possibly have been the period of the biblical ten Plagues of Egypt, according to Michael Oblath's article "Route of Exodus". (2007 Sakenfeld, KD ed. The New Interpreter's Dictionary of the Bible, vol 2, Nashville, Abingdon Press.)

THIRD INTERMEDIATE PERIOD c1069 - 664BCE

21ST TO 25TH DYNASTY

Once again Egypt lost the unity which made her strong. The nation fractured, with Smendes ll the power in the north and the Priests of Amun at Thebes holding sway in the south, barely paying lip service to the pharaoh. There had been an increase of Libyans settling in the Delta and under Shoshenq l, an influx of Libyan princes created what is termed the Bubastite dynasty, which lasted for about 200 years. Their power was broken by an invasion by the Kushite King Piye in c727 BCE, setting the stage for the 25th dynasty – a veritable renaissance of old glories and a reunited empire. Great monuments, including many temples, were built or restored, including the construction of the first pyramids in the Nile Valley since the Middle Kingdom.

However, an old enemy lurked in the shadows. In 671 BCE, the Assyrians began an attack that resulted in constant conflict until the Assyrians, having forced the Kushites out, occupied Memphis and sacked the temples at Thebes.

LATE DYNASTIC PERIOD c664 – 332BCE

26TH – 31ST DYNASTY

After their conquest the Assyrians did not show much interest in their prize and left vassals in charge. These were the Saite kings who allowed increasing Greek influence and expansion into Egypt. This was followed by even more interest from Persia, which actually annexed Egypt from the 27th dynasty. The last indigenous royal house of Egypt ended with King Nectanabo ll and in 332 BCE Persia handed Egypt to Alexander the Great without a whimper. Although he was Greek, Alexander was declared a demigod by the Oracle at Siwa. When he died, his place was taken by his favorite general, Ptolemy.

PTOLEMAIC DYNASTY c332 – 30BCE

This period was named for the Greek general, Ptolemy l (305- 284 BCE). It was Ptolemy who started the great library at Alexandria; his successor, Ptolemy ll, completed its construction. The library was said to hold 70,000 papyrus scrolls and eventually 500,000 early books. Alexandria soon supplanted Memphis as the capital of Egypt and the lighthouse that was built there was one of the seven wonders of the ancient world. The Ptolemaic dynasty did support traditional Egyptian culture, but there was some merging with the Greek pantheon. An example of this was the temple built for the Greek god Serapis.

Egypt was conquered by Rome after the Battle of Actium in 30 BCE, where Marc Anthony and Cleopatra Vll were defeated. The Romans were perhaps less well disposed towards the Egyptians, but all their traditions, including mummification, were tolerated even after the advent of Christianity. It was only in 391 CE that Emperor Theodosius banned any and all pagan rites and closed all the temples. Several were turned into churches but most returned gently, quietly and silently to the sands from which they had come and the gods to whom they had been consecrated.

"Oh Light ! let the Light be kindled for thy Ka, O Osiris Chentamenta. Let the Light be kindled for the Night which followeth the Day : the Eye of Horus which riseth at thy temple: which riseth up over thee and which gathereth upon thy brow ; which granteth thee its protection and overthroweth thine enemies."

Book of the Dead. Spell 275

Chapter Two

Historical Egypt

To the Nile

"Son of the old Moon-mountains African!
Chief of the Pyramid and Crocodile!
We call thee fruitful, and that very while
A desert fills our seeing's inward span:
Nurse of swart nations since the world began,
Art thou so fruitful? or dost thou beguile
Such men to honour thee, who, worn with toil,
Rest for a space 'twixt Cairo and Decan?
O may dark fancies err! They surely do;
'Tis ignorance that makes a barren waste
Of all beyond itself. Thou dost bedew
Green rushes like our rivers, and dost taste
The pleasant sunrise. Green isles hast thou too,
And to the sea as happily dost haste."

John Keats 1795 -182

The Nile: the Egyptians called it "Ar",or "Aur", which meant "black", or "Kemet"; the Black Land or "Ta mery"; the Beautiful One – but mostly they referred to it simply as "the river". It was the Greeks who actually gave the Nile its name, from the word for "valley" i.e. Neilos. The White Nile rises in Lake Victoria in Equatorial Africa, joins the Blue Nile, which rises at Lake Tana in the Ethiopian region of south Sudan and snakes it way down to enter Egypt in the south, at Aswan. From there it sweeps down to the Mediterranean Sea. In historical times it had three phases: Akhet, from June to September, when it was in flood, called the inundation; Peret, from October to February, when all the planting for the year took place; and Shemu, from March to May, when the harvesting was done.

When the river receded after the inundation it left a thick, black layer of incredibly fertile silt – black gold which was planted with emmer wheat for bread and barley for beer, the staple foods. Flax plants to spin for linen and papyrus for many products, including paper, baskets and even small boats, were also economically important. Sugarcane, melons, squashes, pulses, lettuce, leeks, garlic and grapes were also successfully cultivated. There was plenty of land as the river was normally about 2 miles wide; during inundation, it could be anything from 5 to 10 miles across! One could get from Aswan to Alexandria in two weeks by Nile while it was in flood – in the dry season, it would take two months.

Society was very stratified but all were equal before the law. Women had equal rights to men. The bulk of the population were farmers but the land they farmed usually belonged to the local temple. They were paid an average of 5 ½ sacks of grain per month, while a foreman might earn 7 ½ half sacks a month. There was no coinage until the late period, and the size of the grain sack was standardized to facilitate bartering. A standard sack of grain was worth a deben, the equivalent of ninety one grams (3 oz.) of copper or silver. A shirt might cost 5 deben or a cow, 40 deben. The above is just to give you a sense of the times; the bartering system was actually extremely complicated, varied over time and place, and suggests that the working population was generally very poor.

The progress of settlement was dictated by the Nile. Many smaller settlements developed along the length of the river rather than large centers as in other countries. In pre-dynasty and Old Kingdom years, Memphis played the role of the de facto capital; in the 11th and 18th dynasty Thebes played this part, except for a brief period of twenty years when it was at Akhetaten, and in 331 BCE, Alexandria gained and retained the title of capital. In the historical time we are looking at, the real life of the country was played out in the many towns and villages strung along the banks of "the river".

Apart from supplying the water and soil for agriculture, the Nile was also the single greatest source of transportation. Egypt was rich in natural resources; beautiful decorative stones like sandstone, granite and quartz; gold and lead ore; mineral deposits like flint; clay from the river; salt and precious stones like emeralds and amethysts; all these commodities as well as the huge building stones required for the many temples, monuments, tombs and pyramids were shipped up and down the river on flat barges. Egypt was usually able to export grain, gold, linen and papyrus products, the bulk of which would be moved on the river. Richly endowed as it was, Egypt had to import vast quantities of wood, which was shipped along the length of the river. It also imported the very popular blue stone known as lapis lazuli from Afghanistan as well as olive oil, which had to be distributed to all the settlements along the Nile. As you will discern from the timeline above, Egypt prospered during the more or less centralized Old, Middle and New Kingdoms and did less well during the Intermediate times. Additionally, from about 130 BCE Egypt was an important part of the Silk Road, the trade routes established during the Han dynasty in China, and no longer the isolated, insular and inward-looking country of the early dynastic times.

Chapter Three

The Myth Of Creation

*"I am Osiris, the possessor of Maat,
and I subsist by means of it every day."*

Book of the Dead

Now the stage is set to look at Egyptian mythology. Where better to start than at the beginning: the creation of all that is. There are several versions, but all contain most of the elements that occur in this version from the Ennead of Heliopolis Cult. In the beginning there were the dark, swirling waters of chaos called Nu. A mound of land called the Ben Ben rose slowly out of the depth and a god stood upon it. In many versions this was Atum; in some it was Ptah. The god felt his "aloneness" and he mated with his shadow, producing two children. He coughed or spat out Shu, the God of Air (or Wind) and vomited up Tefnut the Goddess of Moisture (or Rain). Atum taught Shu the principles of life and Tefnut learned the principles of order. Shu and Tefnut set out to make the rest of the physical world. Atum was left on Ben Ben contemplating the surrounding chaos. After a while he became concerned for his children and he sent his one eye to find them. When they returned, with his eye, he was so overjoyed he started crying with gratitude; human beings manifested from his tears.

There are two versions of the creation of the earth and the sky. In the first, Shu and Tefnut mate to produce Geb, God of the Earth and Nut, Goddess of the Sky. Shu lifts Nut up and she stretches her body over Geb, forming a beautiful, star-filled canopy over him. In the second version, Geb and Nut also fall in love and mate, but because they are natural brother and sister, Atum is not pleased.

He pushes Nut up into the heavens to keep them apart. Either way there is now enough space for humans to live. Nut was however already pregnant, and she gives birth to 5 children: Osiris, great God of the Earth; Isis, the Queen of the Earth; Set (or Seth), the black sheep of the family - physically speaking I hasten to add – Horus; and Nephthys. Atum is pleased with Osiris, despite the fact that he marries his sister Isis, and leaves the world in his care. Osiris designs the world - i.e. Egypt - with an eye towards perfection: the beautiful river, a wonderful climate and abundant vegetation to answer all the needs of its people. In all things Osiris observes the single, most important principle of the Gods - that of harmony and order and balance in all things. This is known as "Ma'at".

Set became very jealous of Orsiris' success and power. He managed to obtain his exact measurements from his tailor and had a box made to those specifications. The box was beautifully carved and lavishly decorated, and was presented to specially invited guests at the next party. Set announced that the exquisite chest would be given to the one who would best fit inside it. When Osiris lay down in it, it was a perfect fit and Set slammed down the lid, secured it and dropped it in the middle of the Nile. Set announced that Osiris was dead and that he would now rule the world.

Isis was convinced that Osiris was still alive. She set out to find him, and she did, even though the chest that held the body of Osiris had drifted into the sea.

"A flood had cast it upon the land. It had lain in a thicket of young trees. A tree, growing, had lifted it up. The branches of the tree wrapped themselves around it; the bark of the tree spread itself around it; at last the tree grew there, covering the chest with its bark."

The land was Byblos and the tree produced a wonderful fragrance. The King and Queen of Byblos had the tree cut down and incorporated in a column of their palace. Isis approached them and the King had the column taken down and split open, revealing the chest. The royal couple supplied a ship and Isis, "never stirring from beside the chest" returned to Egypt where she hid it. Leaving Nepthys to guard it, Isis set out on a second journey to seek the herbs and other ingredients that would enable her to make the potion that would return Osiris to life. Set realized that Isis had found the chest and he immediately set forth to find out where it was hidden. Nepthys eventually gave up the secret, and when Set retrieved the chest he carved Orsiris' body into forty two (some say fourteen) pieces and scattered them over the length and breadth of Egypt.

Isis wept so bitterly when she returned and Nepthys told her what had happened. Isis set out, yet again, this time to gather together all the parts of her beloved Osiris. To assuage her guilt, Nepthys undertook the journey with her. Wherever they found a body part, they would perform funerary rites and bury the part, building a shrine which would protect it from Set. This is how Egypt was divided into forty two administrative parts or "nomes". The only body part that was not restored was the penis, which had been eaten by a fish.

"Isis then created a replacement part for the phallus and mated with her husband, becoming pregnant with her son Horus."

Orsiris was brought back to life. He became the God of the Underworld and the wise and righteous judge of the dead. Isis gave birth to her son Horus (known as Horus the Younger), who was brought up in secret. When he grew to manhood he did battle with his uncle Set to avenge his father. The war lasted eighty years, but

Horus triumphed in the end; Set was ousted, although he managed to keep control of the deserts. One version of this myth tells the story of the last epic battle where Set, who was a shape-shifter, transformed himself into a rhinoceros as the armies met. Horus was not fooled and he threw his weapon, (curiously enough referred to as a "harpoon") which pierced deeply into the rhino's scull, killing Set. Horus and his mother Isis, ruled the earth together and wisely; in this way "Ma'at", harmony and balance, were restored to the land.

> "I am the Son of Maat, and wrong is what I execrate.
> I am the Victorious one."
>
> Book of the Dead

In this story, as in all the mythology of Egypt, the concept of Ma'at is the primary good, i.e. harmony and balance.

Chapter Four

The Pantheon Of Gods

In order to facilitate discussion of Egyptian religion and mythology, an explanation of the concept of syncretism will be necessary. By definition, syncretism revolves around the concept of the union (or attempted fusion) of different systems of thought or belief (especially in religion or philosophy). Its use in Egyptian mythology applies to the shifting identities of the various Gods and the combinations and borrowings of attributes from one another to create a more appropriate deity. An example of this is the existence of Amun-Ra - a combination of Sky God with Sun God or, in another setting, Ra- Atum, which was a combination of Sun God with Creator God. Another characteristic in Egyptian mythology is the close link between certain gods and specific animals. The connection was often reflected in how the god was represented – usually a human body with an animal head. This form of worship was particularly popular during the Pre-dynastic and Late Dynastic periods. For example: Bastet was originally a lioness and then became a cat; as the Goddess of the Home, she is often shown with a cat's head and holding a "sistrum" which was a sacred rattle. Often there is a kindle of kittens by her side. Thoth, the God of Learning, Magic and Wisdom, is usually depicted with the head of an Ibis and carrying a pen and ink holder.

Ra (Re), the Sun God

One of the most important and beloved Gods. He caused the sun to rise each day and was often seen as the creator of the universe. He had three main aspects as he travelled through the sky in his sunship: Khepri, in the morning; Horakhty at midday and Atem in the afternoon. At night, he travelled through the Underworld. He "died" at the 5th hour, was united with Osiris and "re-born" at the twelfth hour, manifesting as Khepri, as the sun rose. He often fought grueling battles in the night, especially with Apophis, the Demon Snake. There was a strange bond between these two arch-enemies. Some ancient stories say that Apophis was actually Ra's umbilical cord. The Snake would drink the waters of Heaven, creating sandbank obstacles for Ra to navigate. Ra was depicted as a man with a hawk or falcon's head, crowned with a brilliant sun disc that was sometimes encircled by a sacred cobra. His cult was at its height during the New Kingdom.

*"How beautiful is your rising on the horizon,
when you bring dawn to the earth by your radiance.
All the gods rejoice when they see you as king of heaven."*

The Papyrus of Ani

Osiris, God of the Underworld (Duart) and Death

His cult started in the 2nd dynasty and grew strongly, reaching its height in the Middle Kingdom. Having established Egypt, he travelled through the country, teaching life skills, agriculture and how to worship the gods to the people. He left his beloved sister/wife Isis in charge and continued his teaching around the world. He was said to have been born in Thebes, but other myths say he was the city's founder. He was trapped and finally killed by his jealous brother Set, after which he became the beloved lord of the Underworld. This was a fertile and gentle land where all the "righteous dead" lived. He was the judge you faced when you died. There were many festivals in his honor. He was normally depicted as a bearded, mummified human wearing a white, conical crown, trimmed with red ostrich feathers, and surmounted by a small golden disc. He carried a flail and a crook, which was the icon representing divine authority. He often has a green skin indicating his power over vegetation and an ability to resurrect himself. His cult temple is in Abydos where ancient Egyptians believed he was buried.

> "Hail to thee, author of the gods, King of North and South, Osiris, the triumphant one, possessing the entire universe in his beneficent alternations ; He is the Lord of the Universe ;
> Grant me passage in peace. I am righteous, I speak not falsehood knowingly, I am not guilty of duplicity."
>
> Book of the Dead

Isis, Mother of Egypt, Goddess of the Moon, Nature and Fertility

She is closely associated with healing and medicine. She resurrected her husband/brother and healed her son. She was married to her brother Osiris and their love for each other was passionate and enduring; incest was acceptable in many ancient cultures and was seen as a way of maintaining pure, sacred bloodlines. She is often depicted with an empty throne as a headdress, representing the fact that Osiris, who should have been the ruler, was missing. Otherwise her headdress consists of a pair of cow horns encircling a lunar or solar disc. Sometimes she is painted in a yellow hue which is indicative of the indoor life; she is also frequently shown with the beautiful, outspread wings of a kite hawk or a kestrel. One of her icons is a sycamore tree and she is often seen holding her last born child Horus the Younger in her arms. This image is considered to be a forerunner of the pictures of Mary holding the Christ child as her cult remained popular through the 6th century CE. She was warm and compassionate and a beloved goddess of families.

"She who gives birth to heaven and earth,
knows the orphan, knows the widow,
seeks justice for the poor, and shelter for the weak"

Book of the Dead

Set, or Seth, the God of Chaos, Hostility and later on, of Evil

He also held sway over clouds and storms and was associated with the plague. Set had many names: Seth, Seti, Sutech, Setech, Sutech. He was a very complex god and was different from the others in that originally he was regarded as troublesome rather than evil. This changed somewhat after his jealousy of Osiris caused him to kidnap and then kill him and usurp his throne. When Osiris' son, Horus the Younger, set out to avenge his father, the war raged for eighty years – a period in which Set lost part of his leg and his testicles. During this time there was great conflict between the Priests of Horus and the adherents of Set.

Yet it was Set who sat in the prow of Ra's sunboat during his nightly Underworld journeys and fought furious battles with the evil serpent of chaos, Apophis so that the sun might rise the next morning. The idea of duality was an important part of Egyptian mythological belief and the cult of Set stood in strong contrast to the cults of Osiris, Horus and Ra. The pharaohs reluctantly respected him because they regarded him as very powerful.

Set was depicted as a human with a nearly indescribable head. It looked like an aardvark and always shows a curved snout, while the ears are erect and squared off. He often has a forked tail. This was called the Set Animal. Sometimes he was depicted as a greyhound. His sacred animals were many: oryx, antelope, ass, boar, hippopotamus and crocodile. He was often shown in red, holding an "ankh", a cross with a loop above the transverse bar, representing "life" in one hand and a "was" staff in the other. The "was" staff or sceptre was a long stick with a two pronged base and a transverse, angled top, often shaped like a bird or a "Set animal". It was a symbol of authority. During the New Kingdom his cult temple was at Ombos.

At one stage Set was even expelled from Egypt by the other Gods. During his exile he was referred to as Set, the Abominable. By the 2nd Intermediate Period he was closely associated with the Hyskos invaders and subsequent rulers. During this time his cult temple was at Avaris and his consorts were the Hyskos Goddesses Anat and Astarte.

Horus, God of Light, also called God of Kings

"From the very earliest of times, the falcon seems to have been worshipped in Egypt as representative of the greatest cosmic powers. Many falcon gods existed throughout Egypt, though over time, a good number of these assimilated to Horus, the most important of the avian deities. Yet, from all his of many forms, it is nearly impossible to distinguish the "true" Horus. Horus is mostly a general term for a great number of falcon deities." (Dunn, J. See: http://www.touregypt.net/featurestories/horus.htm#ixzz40nyb4xIv)

A most ubiquitous God, he was always depicted either as a falcon, or a man with a falcon head surmounted by a sun disc. The speckled feathers were the stars of heaven and the beating of his wings created the gentle winds. Although he was also a sun god and referred to as the "God of the east," Horus and his link with the sky has more to do with his avian appearance than the sun. He was variously known as; "lord of the sky", "the one on high" and "Horus of the two horizons". In all his forms he has strong associations with light and the power of the sun. In fact his one eye represented the sun while his other the moon. Depending on the source one is using, the sun is the right eye and the moon the left – or the other way around. What is consistent is that in the long battle Horus had with Set to avenge his father's death and reclaim the throne of Egypt, Set clawed out Horus' moon eye and tore it into pieces. The eye was recovered and put together again by the God Thoth, who returned it to Horus; it became the symbol of a "state of soundness". This is known as the "wedjat" or "udjat eye" meaning "the eye that is well". The reigning king of Egypt was regarded as the incarnation of Horus. Thoth, God of Wisdom, Learning, Arts, Magic and Scribe to the Gods.

Thoth also manifested under many names; Tehuty, Djehuty, Tetu and Zehuti to name a few. His cult temple was in the Delta at Hermopolis. As the power of his cult grew, some myths were re-written to proclaim him as the creator God. In the guise of the great Ibis, he was supposed to have laid the egg from which Ra was born. Some say he created himself through the power of his tongue. This is a ghostly presentiment of the beautiful opening of St. John's gospel in the Bible; "In the beginning was the word, and the Word was with God and God was the Word." Thoth is credited with being the inventor of hieroglyphics, arithmetic and astrology, and is usually depicted as carrying a pen and ink or a stylus and palette. He almost always has the head of an Ibis surmounted by the lunar crescent. His other sacred animal is the baboon, a shape he often assumes as well. He is a lunar deity and is called "he who balances"; a reference to his role as the record keeper in the Underworld when the deceased are judged by Osiris. He is known as the epitome of justice, the "Lord of Time" and the "Accountant of the Years". His wife, Seshat, assumes the duties of Ma'at at the judging of the deceased.

There is an air of mystery about him as he is considered to be the author of a book containing "all the secrets of the universe". Owning this book would make the possessor the most powerful sorcerer in the universe. It is called The Book of Thoth or the "emerald tablets of Thoth" and it is said to be hidden in a secret chamber near the Great Pyramid. One of the secrets it will supposedly reveal is that it will prove prove all the gods come from the lost city of Atlantis. Debate about whether these tablets really exist still rages to this day.

Chapter Five

Mythology In Day To Day Ancient Egypt

As a strong example of polytheism, there were about 2,000 gods available for worship in Egypt. Religion guided every aspect of everyday life, from the routine of the Pharaoh down to the laborer working in the fields. The belief was that the only thing that stood between human beings and the total chaos of the universe was the power and goodwill of the gods, who were able to control everything. If the gods were happy the sun would rise, the Nile would flow and the inundation would take place once a year, the crops would flourish and harvests would be fruitful, the seasons would follow one another in an orderly fashion, and there would be peace in the land. Ma'at would prevail; there would be balance and harmony. The rules of societal living were strict and clear.

- The Pharaoh was the absolute Monarch. He was a god or a human or both.

- The King was the head of Government and the military force, and was an incarnation of Horus.

- The Vizier was second in command and administrator of land surveys, the Treasury and building projects. He was also in charge of the Archives.

- There were forty two administrative regions called "nomes", all controlled by governors known as Nomarchs.

However, he real seat of power was the temple. The temples were controlled by the priests, and were were also "the backbone of the economy," as the priests supervised the granaries and were responsible for the collecting and storing of the harvests. They also held the treasures, artifacts and records of the local population.

Priests mostly came from the nobility and they were often professionals as well as officials of the temples. These were the physicians, engineers, architects and teachers who instructed others at the temple's university or school, which was called "The House of Life". Most priests would undertake regular periods as serving priests at the temple. There were four groups, or phyles, of priests. Each group worked three times a year on a one month rotation. Additionally, there were two classes of priests, the first known as "God's servants or prophets", who officiated in the presence of the their god's image and were empowered to interpret the oracles' messages. These "pure ones" carried their god's barque, poured water libations and produced the sacred objects of the cult. For some devotees it would become a full time calling. Next was what was sometimes called the "white kilt class" in recognition of the fact that most of them dressed in unbleached linen. This was an "upper class" consisting of scribes and officials.

However, the bulk of the Egyptian population consisted of farmers, with a good sprinkling of craftsmen and artists among them. Everyone and everything was focused on appeasing the gods and following precise rituals to please, satisfy and glorify the pantheon as a whole. Generally speaking, the gods were considered well disposed and fair but, with having so many, the changing myths, syncretisms, and outside influences of foreign gods during periods of war and occupations, would lead to their demands being overwhelming at times. However, the various and complex ideas were never questioned or even considered contradictory by the general population. Instead they were simply regarded as "layers in the multiple facets of reality" as one Egyptologist has put it. There was usually a central temple in a large town, with several smaller ones as well, each dedicated to a particular main deity but also housing minor deities. Yet every little town, or even a temporary settlement, would have a temple at its center where certain rituals would be followed every day. See Temple Rituals below.

From a theological standpoint, all humans were deemed equal before the law. A human being was made up of discrete "aspects". It is difficult to relate to these aspects – not so much the because of the language but the functions of the aspects; we understand the make-up of a human being very differently today. To the Egyptians, the physical body was khat and had a twin named ka which was an immortal life-force, or the will. The main aspect of the body was the heart, and was considered the seat of emotion, intelligence and moral sense. When the heart was tired the body died and the ka departed to its spiritual origin. The next aspect was the name, which was vitally important as the very foundation of the being. You could not exist without a name, for it was your essence. It is why one might have several names, with each one to match one of the different aspects of your being. Ra had over a hundred different names according to The Book of the Dead; additionally, "he lives whose name is spoken" is an old Egyptian proverb.

Additionally, every body had a "shadow" but it is not clear what purpose it served. It could move independently of the body and did not have to remain in the grave. The next aspect was the ba; it is explained as "the sum of the immortal forces inherent in human beings which made up his personality." Today we might perhaps characterize the ba as the psyche. The final aspect is the akh. This comes into being when the ba and the ka re-unite; at that point, the akh manifests as the "Shining One" and takes its place as a star in the sky.

There is another version of what happens after death, which involves the soul needing to make a difficult journey through the Underworld until it reaches the Hall of Truth. Here the deceased will be judged by Osiris with Horus, Anubis and Thoth at hand, to see if they qualify to live forever in the beautiful Fields of Reeds, where they will enjoy a happier version of life on earth where there is no sickness, no disappointments and no death. This is one of the truly attractive aspects of Egyptian mythology; one is not expected to have led a perfect life. Instead, a balanced life is what is required in line with the expectations of Ma'at; harmony, order, justice, proper conduct. After reciting the forty two negative confessions of all the dreadful things that you have not done, your heart will be weighed on a golden scale against the weight of a white feather to judge how you have spent your time on earth. If your heart is lighter you will go to the Fields of the Reeds. If you fail and your heart is heavier, it will fall off the scale to the floor and be devoured by Amenti, the God with the face of a crocodile, the front of a leopard and the back of a rhinoceros, and your soul will cease to exist. In Egyptian Mythology, there is no hell as a place of torment.

The White Feather

"Given.
Many fear death
Because they already
Feel ridden with sin,
But no man on this earth
Is filled with only white light
Within.
Have more faith
In our Maker,
For our souls and minds
Were created by Him.
Just remember that,
When your deeds
Are measured
By the scale –
The good side
Must outweigh
The bad,
And your heart
Must be as light
As a feather
To win."

Suzy Kassem from Rise Up and Salute the Sun.

Chapter Six

The Central Role Of The Temple And Some Temple Rituals

A temple was consecrated to the central god of the town or village and the god was made accessible in the form of a large image that was kept in a sacred chamber of the temple. All temple rituals were aimed at "maintaining the fabric and process of the universe", and some had to take place at every temple, three times every day. Remember that during the night, Osiris travelled through the Underworld in his barque, frequently in battle with evil forces like Apophis, to ensure that Ra (the sun) would rise, bringing the next day. At every temple, every day, as the sun rose, the priests and assistants would have to bathe, dress and feed the main god and then praise him, thanking him for the new day. Most temples also housed lesser deities as well, and their needs also had to be taken care off. It is important to note that the image of the god was not worshipped. The image was simply a receptacle for the God's ka which was honoured. The daybreak ritual was elaborate, and the priests and other staff would be at the temple long before dawn to prepare a large and substantial first meal for the god. This might include meat, bread, beer, cakes, honey, fruit and vegetables. A small portion is set aside for the god and offered to him as part of the ritual. The rest is divided up between the temple staff once the morning ritual is complete, which often included the following actions:

A fire would be lit and incense burned in the public forecourt of the temple. The temple choir might sing hymns in honor of the god.

The priests proceed to the sealed opening of the god's shrine.

Accompanied by hymns and burning incense the clay or mud seal was broken.

The cord around the doorknobs was untied.

The priest would call out, representing the king: "It is the king who has sent me to see the god."

Light from the rising sun is introduced to the face of the god

On "seeing" the god, the priest would kiss the ground, raise his arms while singing, and then prostate himself, stretching his arms out in front of him to lie on his stomach.

Gifts of incense, oil or honey are offered.

The previous day's offerings are removed.

The priest's hands are purified before he touches and bathes the god

The god is dressed in four new lengths of cloth; white; blue; green and then blue once more.

He is offered scented oil and his face is painted with green (copper) and black (lead) eye paint.

An offering, perhaps a small statue, personifying Ma'at and "What is Right" is offered.

A very small selection from the meal is placed before the image. The "essence" of the meal is what the god requires.

The priest withdraws from the shrine, moving backwards and

erasing his footprints as he goes.

Offerings of natron, incense and fresh water are left behind.

The chamber is resealed and locked.

Each part of this ritual had specific words that had to be repeated every time the ritual is performed, although there were many versions of what is required. These were referred to as formulas. After the main god has been honored, variations of these duties were performed for the lesser gods who might have also been housed in the temple. These rituals had to be performed three times a day in every temple, no matter how big or small. It has been noted that the midday and sunset rituals were not usually so elaborate, but had to be performed nonetheless.

The ordinary people were not allowed access the inner sanctuary of the temple, so the priests had to devise other, meaningful ways to allow them access to their gods. To this end there was a calendar of religious festivals arranged for the year at the larger religious centers. The highlight of such a festival would be a parade of the priests carrying the god in a shrine through the streets on a specially prepared and gorgeously decorated barque. These festivals were important and strengthened the link between the ordinary people and the gods. The ordinary person was also given the opportunity to consult the god as an Oracle at this time. Certain stops along the way would be selected where the barque would be set down and the god would be revealed. If you had a pressing problem you could write it down in the form of a question that could be answered by a "yes" or a "no" and present it to the priest, who would then present it to the god. The questions could be written on a flake of limestone called an ostraca, or rolled up on a small piece of papyrus and placed in something else, such as an amulet. "You would get your answer from the God who would move forwards or backwards depending on if the answer were "yes" or "no". The parade would be followed by a feast for the people supplied by the god. One of the largest such feasts on record lasted 27 days during which 3,694 loaves of bread, 410 cakes and 905 jars of beer were happily consumed! Of course there would also be less elaborate festivals at all the local villages along the Nile. Individuals would also have shrines or special places set aside for their favorite and domestic gods in their homes or gardens. Personal piety was regarded as very important; it seems from historical writings that have survived to this day that most Egyptians saw themselves living in a world with many dangers. In the New Kingdom, it became the fashion to build a special room at the rear of the formal temple for private prayer for ordinary citizens. They were rooms were aptly referred to as the "chapel of the Hearing Ear".

Chapter Seven

Sources Of The History Of Egyptian Mythology

Egyptian civilization is over 3,000 years old and the language is the second oldest in the world. Its origin is northern Afro-Asiatic and it is related to both the Berber and Semitic languages. It was written in the form of logograms (where a picture stood for a word) called hieroglyphics. The first example of hieroglyphics was discovered in a pre-dynastic tomb in Abydos and date from about 3200 BCE.

Formal script was used mainly on monuments like the pyramids and made exclusive use of hieroglyphics. This form of writing took a long time to produce and required knowledge and skill. A simpler, cursive form called hieratic and more suitable for writing on papyrus evolved for religious texts and routine record keeping. This was followed by the even more simplified demotic style in the 7th century BCE, used for business and literary texts.

Most of what we have pieced together of the mythology of Egypt comes from the extensive writings inside the passages and burial chambers of the discovered pyramids. Collectively they are known as the Pyramid and Coffin texts. This collection was started in 1881 (or 1880 depending on what source you consult) when Gaston Maspero discovered the Pyramid of King Unas from the 5th dynasty. These examples were all hieroglyphic funerary texts and also what seemed like autobiographical notes. Another such tomb was the one Pharaoh Teti (6th dynasty) built for himself at Saqqara. The inside was like an art gallery of sculptures with detailed descriptions of the daily life in Egypt during the Old

Kingdom. In the early 19th century a papyrus written by an author known only as Ipuwer was found describing a period in Egyptian history that might well have been the time of the plagues and the biblical Exodus. There is an astonishing website which documents Egyptian historical findings over time, the latest ones being in February 2016.

It can be found at: http://www.crystalinks.com/egyptnews.html

The Rosetta Stone

Despite the plethora of texts available, progress on translating Egyptian hieroglyphs was painfully slow thanks to the difficulty of deciphering the texts. This obstacle vanished with the discovery of the Rosetta Stone, which "changed everything" to use a popular phrase. It was a black basalt stone first found by Lieutenant Pierre-François Bouchard, an officer in Napoleon's invasion force, among the ruins of Fort St. Julion at the mouth of the Nile in 1799. The stone was turned over to Britain when Napoleon was defeated and Alexandria capitulated in 1801. This stone has one text on it, repeated in three different scripts: once in hieroglyphics (14 lines); once in demotic (32 lines) and once in Greek (54 lines). It was like a key to unlock the meaning of the hieroglyphics.

Scholars immediately set their sights on breaking the hieroglyphic code. This honor finally went to Jean-Francois Champollion (1790-1832) in 1822. The content of the Rosetta Stone itself was not very exciting, as it turned out to be a decree issued by a panel of priests assembled in honour of Pharaoh Ptolemy V Epiphanes, King of Egypt, in 195 BCE. It is the forerunner of an "annual report" and stones like this would have been displayed in the open forecourt of the local temple as a "report back" to the constituents. It enumerated events during his reign: taxes collected; privileges extended; an exceptional Nile inundation in the 8th year of his reign and subsequent planning for a dam; generous gifts to certain temples and grateful subjects demanding a statue be erected in his honor with the following plaque: "Ptolemy, the Savior of Egypt".

The Book of the Dead

The single most informative source of Egyptian mythology and mysticism we have is a collection of texts and spells in the so-called "Book of the Dead". This is a selection of formulae for securing eternal life for the elite of Egyptian society through specific burial practices. Most of these instructions date from the New Kingdom to the end of the Ptolemaic period. Copies have been found in various versions, with the first existing in five copies, inscribed in hieroglyphics on the walls and passages of the pyramids of kings at Sakkâra and in tomb inscriptions, sarcophagi, coffins, stelae and papyri from c2133 BCE to 200 CE. These were edited by the priests of the College of Annu. A second copy on papyrus and in hieroglyphics is known as the Theban version, and was much used during the 18th to the 20th dynasty. A third, very similar version is also on papyrus, written in hieroglyphics and hieratic script, and was in use in the 20th dynasty. The fourth version, known as the Saïte version, is also in hieroglyphs and hieratic script, and was used from the 26th dynasty till the end of the Ptolemaic period. A complete copy of The Book of the Dead can be found online at: https://archive.org/stream/egyptianbookofde00reno/egyptianbookofde00reno_djvu.txt

The Skabaka Stone

Another source of information, though somewhat at odds with traditional thought at the time, is the Skabaka Stone. It is green breccia basalt stone, approximately 137 x 93cm, kept at the British Museum, but of unknown provenance. It is named after the Kushite Pharaoh Skabaka, who had discovered a worm-eaten papyrus found while inspecting an old temple in c716 – 702 BCE, and had its contents copied onto the stone. It has three sections: the first is known as the Memphis Theogany and is an alternative version of the creation of the world. It explains that the God Ptah brought the world into being through his heart and his words, much like the Christian God in the biblical Genesis. The second story concerns the long war between Horus and Seth which is brought to an end by mutual peacemaking - not by a great battle in which Horus defeats Seth.

"Reed and papyrus were placed on the double door of the House of Ptah.
That means Horus and Seth, pacified and united. They fraternized so as to cease quarrelling
in whatever place they might be, being united in the House of Ptah,
the "Balance of the Two Lands" in which Upper and Lower Egypt had been weighed."

From the Skabaka Stone.

The third story is about Osiris' body being washed out on the shore of Memphis and his body having been buried there rather than in the traditional Abydos.

Chapter Eight

The Underworld And Life After Death

There were always elaborate burial customs among the Pharaohs and the upper classes in Egypt. The poor however were usually buried in the desert where their remains were well preserved due to the prevailing dry weather conditions. The rich were usually buried in stone tombs, called mastaba, and the gods of course in their temples. It was the excellent condition of the skeletons retrieved from the desert that spawned the idea of mummification which reached its height in the New Kingdom. The Egyptians did not see death as finality but rather an interruption of life in this world in preparation for a happier life in the underworld. When the khat died the ka departed, leaving the ba and body behind. The body had to be preserved because eventually the ka would return to unite with the ba so that the akh could start its journey to the underworld. For this reason the person was buried with certain necessities: food; drink; clothing; some valued objects; some amulets or ornaments, sometimes even with a little barque for transport and often with little wooden figures called ushabty. Ushabty literally means "answerers"; they would take care of any duties that the deceased person might have to undertake in the Underworld. Of course there would also be many formulae buried with the travellers, carved on stone or written on papyri to ensure a safe journey.

The priests would perform the embalming and mummification. The process took 70 days. The internal organs were taken out of the lower left side of the body. Some descriptions say the heart was never removed and some indicate that only part of the heart was taken out, the rest was left in situ. The brain was extracted through the nose using a long bronze hook. The body and organs would all be desiccated by lying in a salt mixture called natron. Thereafter the organs would be sealed into canopic jars. The rest of the body would be treated with spices and perfumes. A heart scarab would be inserted next to what remained of the heart and then the body would be carefully wrapped in bandages of flaxen cloth. Formulae, prayers, charms and personal possessions might be placed next to the skin or in the folds of the bandages and the bandaged body would be smeared with gum. The body would be laid in a sarcophagus and be taken to the final resting place on a sled in a procession. On reaching the grave, the priest would perform a ritual called "opening the mouth" which would supposedly reanimate the mummy and send it on its way through the Underworld. The tomb would then be sealed. Initially the jars containing the body parts would be placed close to the mummy but, by the 21st dynasty the body parts were reinserted in the body before it was wrapped.

Chapter Nine

Pyramids And Their Locations

The pyramids are the largest physical remnants we have of any ancient civilization, the easiest to explain, yet the most difficult to understand. It's obvious that they are the final resting places of highly important individuals, but the mysteries of their construction – and how they were aligned so precisely with the aid of astronomy – leave us with more questions than answers. Like anything the Egyptians did, there were many rituals surrounding the building of a pyramid tomb. The first ritual, dating back to the 2nd dynasty, was called "stretching the cord" and it was done at night. The building was precisely aligned by careful astronomical observations. There are several ways in which this could have been done. A tool called a "market" or "merket" could have been used. This is a notched stick through which the Great Bear constellation could be viewed; this would have allowed architects to calculate true North, where a central maker was driven into the ground. The King would then stand opposite the Goddess Seshat, each holding a vertical pole linked together by a loop of rope. They would stretch out the rope and mark the four corners of the building by driving marker stakes into the ground. The priests would then hoe the foundation trench and mould a mud brick, which would sometimes be inscribed, and place it with any other "deposits" to be included in the foundation. A thin layer of Nile sand was poured into the trench and workmen would take over the task of filling the foundations. A large stone block would be placed in one corner at the start of the construction phase.

Once the construction was complete, the building had to be purified before it could be dedicated to the one who would be buried within. The purification ritual was called "the strewing of the besen" and would involve the spreading of gypsum or natron throughout the construction. The temple would then be dedicated to the particular god who would live or be buried there. This was always accompanied by one of the most important religious rituals: "the opening of the mouth". This ritual would allow the deceased to continue living in the Underworld. The mummy would first be purified using natron and cow's milk. The Kehrheb, or priest conducting the ceremony, then performed the transmutation ritual which would turn the food offerings into spiritual food. He would then touch the mouth, eyes, ears and nose to awaken the senses and allow the deceased to partake of the essence of the food and drink which would be supplied regularly. Slits would be made in the bandages using the embalmer's tools: a ritual adze; a peseshkaf, which was a spooned blade and a sharper, serpent-headed blade. The entire ritual consisted of 75 episodes, accompanied by many spells or formulas, songs, flowers and the burning of sacred oils and incense. The sarcophagus or image would then be sealed in an inner chamber.

When scholars try to answer the question of why the pyramids have their triangular design and why they are so precisely located, the field becomes highly controversial. One romantic suggestion is that the apex of the structure would bring the person as close to the sky as possible. Why would that be so important? There are about 80 pyramids still standing in Egypt, and the most impressive are the three located at Giza, from the 4th dynasty. The largest was built by Pharaoh Khufu. Its base is 13 acres, is composed of 2,300,000 stone blocks and contains 3 burial chambers – and it is perfectly aligned with Orion and true North. It's also precisely 20 degrees Celsius inside. The cornerstones have an advanced ball and socket construction that deals effectively with heat expansion and earthquakes. There is an excellent video you will enjoy watching available online at:

https://www.youtube.com/watch?v=rcKahraBiBY

This sets out in detail the eight engineering feats that seem to be way beyond the skills of the Ancient Egyptians to scholars today. There are some aspects of the construction that these scholars say would be impossible to duplicate even today with our advanced technology.

Conclusion

The Egyptians did have extensive knowledge of the skies. This was how the priests were able to "predict" the inundation of the Nile. When they saw the star Sirius rise just before the sun, they knew the annual flood was imminent. This also became the marker for the Summer Solstice and the beginning of their new year. The statue of Isis at Dendera was precisely oriented to the returning of Sirius so that at the first heliacal rising, the jewel placed on her forehead would catch the light and glitter. So many of the Egyptian structures were sighted and constructed in such a way that the first rays of the rising sun would touch the Image of the god, even where it was ensconced in an inner chamber. This was in celebration of Ra having made another successful night time journey through the Underworld, bringing another day and keeping their world safe against the return of chaos.

A Sphinx

"Close-Mouthed you sat five thousand years and never let out a whisper.
Processions came by, marchers, asking questions you answered with grey eyes never blinking, shut lips never talking.
Not one croak of anything you know has come from your cat crouch of ages.
I am one of those who know all you know and I keep my questions: I know the answers you hold."

Carl Sandburg

Made in the USA
Lexington, KY
20 September 2016